Real Estate Through Airbnb Rental Arbitrage

The Beginner's Guide to Earning a Sustainable, Passive Income Without Owning Any Property (Traditional Buy & Hold Doesn't Work Anymore)

Phil C. Senior

© Copyright 2019 - All rights reserved.

The content contained within this book may not be reproduced, duplicated nor transmitted without direct written permission from the author or the publisher.

Under no circumstances will any blame or legal responsibility be held against the publisher or author for any damages, reparation, or monetary loss due to the information contained within this book, either directly or indirectly.

Legal Notice:

This book is copyright protected. It is only for personal use. You cannot amend, distribute, sell, use, quote or paraphrase any part of the content within this book without the consent of the author or publisher.

Disclaimer Notice:

Please note the information contained within this document is for educational and entertainment purposes only. All effort has been executed to present accurate, up to date, reliable, and complete information. No warranties of any kind are declared or implied. Readers acknowledge that the author is not engaging in the rendering of legal, financial, medical or professional advice. The content within this book has been derived from various sources. Please consult a licensed professional before attempting any techniques outlined in this book.

By reading this document, the reader agrees that under no circumstances is the author responsible for any losses, direct or indirect, that are incurred as a result of the use of information contained within this document, including, but not limited to: Errors, omissions, or inaccuracies.

You may also like these books:

Real Estate Investing Through Tax Liens & Deeds: The Beginner's Guide To Earning Sustainable A Passive Income While Reducing Risks (Traditional Buy & Hold Doesn't Work Anymore)

Blogging For Profit: The No Nonsense Beginner's Blueprint To Earn Money Online With Your Blog

Badass Passive Income Ideas That Your Teacher Won't Tell You: Multiple Income Streams (Both Online And Offline) That Will Help You Achieve Financial Freedom And Money Goals

Introduction to Airbnb — *12*

Chapter 1: Beginning Your Airbnb Journey — *17*

Benefits of Airbnb Investing — 17

Airbnb Is Part of a Growing Market — 18
You Can Create an Automated System — 18
You Can Have Units All Over the United States — 19
You Can Expand into Other Real Estate — 19
Interaction with People from All over the World — 20
Potential Earnings — 20

Factors to Consider — 21

Chapter 2: Potential Risks — *24*

Safety — 24

Managing Strangers — 25
Communicate on the Main Airbnb Site — 26

Competition Is Fierce — 27

Bad Tenants — 29

Legal Problems — 31

Risk of Vacancy — 32

Chapter 3: Location Research — *34*

Market Research — 36

AirDNA — 37
Identify Your Competition — 38
Understanding Listings — 39

Best and Worst U.S. Cities for Airbnb — 41

Best Places for One- and Two-Bedroom Properties ___42
Worst Places for One Bedroom Properties _____42
Worst Place for Two Bedroom Properties._____43

Chapter 4: Hidden Expenses _____*44*

Thinking of All Your Expenses _____44
Keys _____45
Furnishing Your Airbnb _____46
Bills and Taxes _____47
Cleaning Services _____48

Hidden Structural Problems _____49

Chapter 5: Striking an Agreement with the Landlord _____*52*

Tips for Talking to Your Landlord _____53
Make Your First Impression Great_____53
Know Guidelines and Rules_____54
Airbnb Community _____55
How Do Your Neighbors Feel? _____55
Always Remain Calm and Understanding _____56
Consider Their Position _____56

Tips for Handling the Agreement _____57
Be Willing to Negotiate _____58
Control Your Emotions_____58

How Would You React?_____59

Chapter 6: Furnished vs. Unfurnished Units __*60*

Furnished _____60

Function of the Furniture	62
Decorating	63

Unfurnished — 65

Chapter 7: Understanding the Neighbors — 67

Tips When Talking to Your Neighbors — 68

Understand Your Neighbors	68
Ask Your Neighbors to Meet with You	69
Have a Neighborhood Meeting	70
Talk About Safety	71
Offer Notice of Guests	72
Be Honest About Claims	72

Visualization Exercise — 73

Chapter 8: Making the Unit Airbnb Ready — 75

Steps and Tips to Prepare Your Home — 75

1. Keep Your Eyes Open for Safety — 76
2. Clean Before Photographs — 77
3. Don't Have Anything Out That You Don't Want Your Guests to Touch — 78
4. Stop Your Mail — 79
5. Provide a Check-In for When You Are Not There — 79
6. Provide Brochures and Menus — 80
7. Equip Your Airbnb for Its Guests — 81

Visualization Exercise — 83

Chapter 9: What About Insurance? — 85

Airbnb Insurance — 86

Host Protection Insurance	87
Host Guarantee	88

Renter's and Homeowner's Insurance — **89**

Chapter 10: A How-to in Advertising — *91*

Personal Profile — **91**
- Profile Picture — 92
- A Description About You — 92

Taking Photographs — **93**

Writing Powerful Descriptions — **95**

Description Exercise — **97**

Listing the Airbnb — **98**

Chapter 11: Airbnb Ranking Tips — *100*

Ranking Tips — **101**
- Use a Guest Welcome Book — 101
- Don't be Afraid to Over-Deliver — 102
- Make Sure to Update Your Calendar Daily — 103
- Always Respond Within the Hour — 104
- Think Like a Guest — 105
- Cancel as Few Bookings as Possible — 106
- Don't Become Too Competitive with Pricing — 107
- Have Guests Add Your Listing to their Wishlists — 108

Chapter 12: Managing Your Airbnb — *109*

Automating the Check-In Process and Tools — **109**
- Automated Check-In — 110
- Use the Airbnb Management Software — 111

Guest Relations _____ 111

Cleaning Team and How to Outsource Efficiently
_____ 112

Generating 5-Star Reviews _____ 113

Chapter 13: Scaling Up the Business _____ *116*

Tips for Growing Your Business _____ 116

Manage Your Risk _____ 117
Have a Strong Business Plan _____ 118
Don't Spend Too Much Time Worrying _____ 119
Have Multiple Listings _____ 120
Be Reasonable About Paying Your Staff _____ 120

Chapter 14: Mindset _____ *122*

The Winning Mindset _____ 123

Maintain a Calm Environment _____ 124
Have a Passion to Succeed _____ 125
You are Always Looking for Ways to Grow _____ 125
You Watch Your Spending _____ 126
Monitor the Progress of Your Goals _____ 127
Always Think Positively _____ 127
Surround Yourself with Like-Minded People _____ 128

Conclusion _____ *131*

References _____ *137*

Introduction to Airbnb

If you feel like you are struggling to start your Airbnb journey, you have come to the right place. Through this guide, you will learn how to grow your idea into a reality.

The real estate business seems to be the way to go for investing, especially if you want a passive income. There are many types of real estate that people invest in, but one of the newest topics is the Airbnb. First established in 2008 by a couple of designers, Airbnbs have grown intensely over the last decade. It does not matter if you are vacationing with your family for a week, or you are a traveling nomad looking for your next place to hang your hat — one of the first places people choose to look into is an Airbnb.

There is a lot of room for growth with the high interest of the Airbnb. However, vacationers will not have a place to stay if people don't invest in Airbnb real estate. This book will help you discover your potential as an Airbnb host. You will learn to think like your guest, whether they are a vacationer, on a business trip for a couple of days, or a digital nomad wishing to stay for a few months.

Chapter 1 starts off with the basics. You will learn the benefits of an Airbnb, its potential earnings, and the other factors to consider. Chapter 2 will then bring you to the risks of running an Airbnb. This is an important topic, as you need to understand the risks so you can protect yourself and your business.

Chapter 3 starts to go into more detail about the beginning of the Airbnb process by talking about location research. This is an important step, and one that you need to make sure you spend time on. Along with the location, the hidden expenses can also cause stress to your new business. Chapter 4 will help you think about all of your expenses, and how to prepare for them.

Getting other people on board with your idea can be one of the biggest challenges to have, especially if you don't own the unit in which you want to turn into an Airbnb. If you rent your location, you have to speak to your landlord. Chapter 5 will teach you how to get your landlord on board.

To make your Airbnb furnished or unfurnished? This is often the question beginners—even experts — ask. If you decide to furnish your Airbnb, what are the steps you will need to take? There are a few tips to help you with this process in Chapter 6.

Chapter 7 will take a dive into how to talk to your neighbors about your Airbnb idea. Just like you need to have patience with your landlord, you may need more patience with your neighbors. You need to understand that your neighbors are worried about their families and homes. However, through the tips you receive, you can make sure to give your neighbors the best of their time.

You now have your landlord on board, and your neighbors agree to the Airbnb and are comfortable with the idea. You have furnished your unit, and now it is time to make your unit Airbnb ready. But, you are wondering... *how do I go about doing this*? Chapter 8 will help you with this process. You will receive steps and tips that will allow you to prepare your unit.

One of the biggest factors to consider is insurance. This is a challenge when it comes to many people, because they don't know what insurance is the best for them. Fortunately, Chapter 9 will help you learn all about Airbnb insurance. There are two main types, and it is a good idea to look into both of them. Of course, you don't want to forget about renter's and homeowner's insurance, depending on whether you rent or own your unit.

Once you have your insurance set and your Airbnb is ready to go, it is time to create your Airbnb profile.

Chapter 10 will help you with this process by walking you through the steps to create your profile, taking photographs of your unit, and writing a powerful description.

Once your Airbnb is open and ready for business, it is time to focus on your ranking. While you never want to become overly concerned about your ranking, you want to make it to the top of people's search engines on the Airbnb website. This will make you more visible. However, to do this, you need to understand what factors go into deciding who is ranked at the top. Chapter 11 will not only discuss this, but you will receive tips to help you reach the top rank.

Other than ranking, you need to manage your Airbnb, too. Chapter 12 will help you with this process by discussing automated systems, guest relations, and generating 5-star reviews. Even when your Airbnb is up and ready, there is still a lot of work to get done! Of course, you always want to grow your business, and this is when Chapter 13 comes in. You will receive tips to help you expand your business and build the Airbnb empire that you dream of.

It is important to know that none of this will be possible without your winning mindset. But what is the winning mindset? You will learn about this is Chapter 14. You will receive tips to help you achieve and maintain the winning mindset, so you can reach your full potential as an Airbnb host.

Chapter 1: Beginning Your Airbnb Journey

Over the last few years, Airbnb has become a common choice for people looking to invest in the real estate market. Part of this is because of the vacationers interested in more value and privacy than a hotel has to offer. Another part is because of the increase in the digital nomad lifestyle – people who want to travel throughout the world as cheaply as possible. But, these are not the only reasons for the growing popularity of Airbnb rentals.

Benefits of Airbnb Investing

Airbnb is part of the short-term rental market that is quickly growing all around the world. Even though Airbnbs struggled to prove themselves worthy in real estate, investors quickly noticed several advantages of Airbnb.

Airbnb Is Part of a Growing Market

Over the last decade, short-term investing has grown rapidly. They are making more money than long-term rentals and are also affordable. If there is growth within the market, you will find personal growth. You will learn new skills as a host for an Airbnb. You will learn about finances, advertising, and customer service. Airbnb investing will allow you to take steps toward furthering your investing career.

You Can Create an Automated System

There is a lot of software that Airbnb hosts can use to make their lives easier, especially if they have a lot of properties to manage. While they will hire staff, such as a cleaning team and property managers, hosts still need to keep everyone on board, and many like to build guest relations themselves and not leave this to their staff. The Airbnb software will automatically book a reservation, set up schedules for your staff, and help you keep on track with your tasks. On top of this, you can quickly read your reviews and note any changes that you need to make in your processes.

You Can Have Units All Over the United States

If you live in the United States, you can establish Airbnbs in several states, and manage each one through your staff, the Airbnb software, and by keeping your processes the same throughout. This will allow you to grow your business into a six-figure salary. By building your Airbnb empire, you can establish a passive income that will allow you to visit your units on your own time and also help your staff when needed.

You Can Expand into Other Real Estate

You may start with the Airbnb, but have plans to develop into other forms of real estate. For example, you may start flipping homes and turning them into Airbnbs, or sell them for a profit. You might purchase rental units, such as condos and apartments, and manage these buildings. There are a lot of skills that you can learn as a host for Airbnbs that you won't learn with other forms of real estate. This can help you develop in several ways, including giving you the confidence to pursue other interests.

Interaction with People from All over the World

The people you will meet as a host will be from all over the world. You will meet people from different backgrounds who are willing to share their stories. They will broaden your knowledge of other cultures and bring more creativity into your life. You will learn more than you thought possible from your guests. You may even get repeat customers on an annual basis! The stronger skills you provide as a host, the more appreciation you will receive from your guests.

Potential Earnings

As long as you are cautious of the way you manage your property and find a great location, you will receive financial benefits. You might feel that you are struggling on the financial side when you first start your Airbnb, but the more work you put into advertising, managing, and guest relations, the more prosperous your rental will become.

Each Airbnb will produce their own earnings. For example, some places only make $500 a month, while other people see close to $10,000. On average, hosts make about $900 every month (Leasca, 2017). Of course, you need to realize that your income will vary from month to month. For example, you may have more guests during the summer months of June, July, and August than any other time of year. Therefore, you will earn more during these months.

Factors to Consider

While Airbnb investing has tons of great benefits, there are still factors to consider before you take the leap into this type of real estate investing.

1. **You need to start slow.** Starting slow is the best advice for any investor. By going at a slower pace, you will make less mistakes and learn what works for you and what doesn't. You can gain a better understanding of your

guests, such as what draws them in and what keeps them out.

2. **Expenses can jump out at you.** If you own a home, you'll understand there are surprise expenses from time to time. The same goes for someone who invests in real estate. You may get a call in the middle of the night saying the central air is not working. You need to be aware of these surprise expenses and have a plan of action for when they happen.

3. **Your safety.** You are going to think of the safety of your guests, but this doesn't mean you forget about your own safety. Listing your Airbnb does leave you open to several risks.

4. **Setting your price.** The price you want to set for your Airbnb in your head may not be the best price. People want cheap when they are traveling and staying at an Airbnb. Their version of "cheap" may not be your version of "cheap". You always need to monitor prices of other Airbnbs. Don't set a price and stick to it. You may need to increase or decrease pricing for special events or certain times of the year. Be prepared to change your prices.

5. **Research.** One of the biggest steps you will take before opening your Airbnb is the

research process. You want to have a thorough understanding of Airbnbs. You need to know the laws, your rights, and the rights of your guests.

6. **What are your goals?** Why do you want to open an Airbnb? What are your goals for this chapter in your life? Everyone has different goals, and you need to keep your goals in your desk drawer. For example, are you saving up for retirement? Are you interested in making real estate investing your career?

Take time in this section to write down your goals. Even if you are not sure your goals at this moment, write down some ideas that you have. Ask yourself, "Why Airbnb renting?" or "What are my goals?" You can even take this time to sort out your thoughts.

_____
_____
_____
_____
_____
_____
_____
_____
_____
_____

Chapter 2: Potential Risks

No one wants to think about the risks that are associated with their new career or hobby. However, it is essential — especially for Airbnb investing.

Safety

When it comes to your Airbnb, guests, yourself, neighbors, and any employees, you want their safety to be your top priority. This can be stressful for many people, especially in the beginning. There is a lot to think about when it comes to the safety of everyone. But, the more you realize safety is number one, the easier it is to come up with rules, guidelines and procedures, and handle any situation calmly and rationally.

Managing Strangers

You need to realize that you will manage people you don't know. While most people you will meet are friendly and respectful, there are always people who will not care about your Airbnb. They will not show respect to you or your rental. You want to make sure you have rules and guidelines in place that you and your staff follow. You also want emergency numbers close by, or a way to notify the police, such as an alarm, if something bad happens.

Make sure you have any house rules in place before you start accepting guests. Allow them to view your rules before they agree to stay at your Airbnb. This will ensure that your guests understand the rules and agree to all of your terms. For example, inform them of whether smoking is allowed, how the laundry facilities work, any kitchen rules, if you allow burning of candles, etc.

You also need to think about your guests' intentions. Are they on vacation for a week, the summer, or just one night? Are they digital nomads who work online and looking for a place to stay for a few days? Whether you are renting a room in your home, or you have a small house you rent and stay close by, you need to think about the reasons for why they are interested in your Airbnb. Unfortunately, with the growth of Airbnbs, a lot of people have started using them to their advantage. Hosts have dealt with robbery and other bad and scary situations. Get to know the people who want to stay at your Airbnb as much as possible before any forms are signed.

This safety factor is not meant to cause anxiety nor scare you from establishing an Airbnb. For the majority of the time, hosts have great experiences with their guests and they hope to meet again. Some guests maintain contact with their hosts after they leave. Investing in any rental property brings up the risks of safety. As long as you work through the Airbnb website, set your house rules, and make sure that safety is your number one priority, you will have great guests.

Communicate on the Main Airbnb Site

You should always communicate with people through the trusted Airbnb messaging system. Through this system, you are protected from cancellations, refunds, and other problems that could arise. While you have to follow the Airbnb terms of service and payment terms of service, these guidelines are here to help you and your guests. You want everyone to have a positive experience at your Airbnb, and this is one way to ensure that that happens as much as possible.

This site allows you to see your guests' profile and receive profile verification. You can request that your guests use this, as it allows you to make sure they are who they say they are. You can receive information about your guests, such as their government issued IDs, email addresses, Facebook profiles, and phone numbers.

The steps are fairly easy to follow to add verification to your account. This is also something that all hosts will want to do for their Airbnb. To verify your account, you need to follow these three steps (What are profile verifications and how do I get them?, n.d.):

1. Go to Airbnb.com and hit "profile."
2. Select "trust and verification."
3. Select a verification to add under the section "add more verification."

Competition Is Fierce

With a quickly growing market, competition is fierce in the Airbnb world. There are nearly 3 million listings for Airbnbs in over 65,000 cities (Khoury, 2018). This brings a lot of competition, especially for people who live in larger areas with a lot of tourism. The best way to get your Airbnb noticed is to make it stand out. You want to do something that is slightly different from all other Airbnbs in your area. For example, you can lower your price a bit, or offer features that most Airbnbs do not. You can even offer a special discount to guests who leave reviews, whether this is 15% off their next stay, or that they will receive a gift card.

You will also want to spend a little more money than planned fixing up your rental. Don't buy the cheapest bedding. Go all out when it comes to the comfort of your guests. Make sure that your Airbnb is clean, and everything you offer is stocked and available. Another tip is to provide brochures to businesses in your community. Some businesses may even make a deal with you that, if someone stays in your Airbnb, they receive a special discount. Get as creative, as you need to make sure you stand out from your competition, but don't allow yourself to struggle financially.

Bad Tenants

Once you start your research on investing in an Airbnb, you will read a lot of horror stories about bad tenants. This is a risk with every rental property, and something that needs preparation. For example, you will want to make sure you have insurance and complete background checks of your tenants, especially if you are staying in the Airbnb at the same time as them.

While you are covered under the Airbnb Host Protection Concierge, once you sign up, this does not cover every single incident that can happen. Tenants may stay longer than they signed up for, causing problems for your next tenants. They may also damage property or steal from you. Sometimes, you will not notice everything they do right away. Your next tenant might tell you about it, or, one day, you may be walking around your Airbnb and notice an object missing. You don't know when it disappeared. This might seem a bit strange, but your mind gets used to objects sitting around. If you are not paying attention to the object, your mind will naturally assume it is there until you become more mindful and wonder what happened to it, or how long it's been gone.

Some bad tenants are disrespectful and dishonest. For example, a couple rents from you for two months. You do your best to give them a pleasant experience, but they never seem to be truly happy with your service. Once they leave, they take time to write a negative review about your Airbnb. They state that you didn't keep the place clean, you became rude, and they felt unwelcomed.

Unfortunately, you can't defend yourself with negative reviews. Instead, you need to note what is said and analyze their stay. If you did everything you could for them, move on from the review. Focus on your past tenants who left positive reviews and future tenants. Even though the negative review is in the open for everyone to read, one negative review generally doesn't keep people away. Most people who are searching for their next Airbnb realize that some people are naturally rude. They look at several, perhaps all, of your reviews, and decide if your place is their best choice.

You can try to do everything in your power to prevent bad tenants, but there is never a guarantee that it will work. You never know who a person truly is until they have signed all the forms and are staying at your Airbnb. This is why you always want to remember to be on guard and protect yourself and your business as much as possible. However, you don't want to fall into the mindset that someone can be bad or dangerous. Take the necessary precautions, but expect people to be kind and respectful.

Legal Problems

If there are people who dislike Airbnbs, it is people who own and run hotels. Since the Airbnb made headlines in 2008, people have started to stay in Airbnbs instead of hotels. This means, especially in some areas, hotels are losing their guests at a rapid rate. Many hotels know that their numbers are declining, and they blame the Airbnbs.

Many hotels brought this issue up in a legal way, and did whatever they could to restrict access to Airbnbs in certain areas. These restrictions are a risk to Airbnbs. When you are setting up your location, you want to work closely with the city, county, and state. You want to make sure that you are following all the rules, guidelines, and restrictions for your area. If you don't, you will face charges or receive a fine. The city can even ask you to close your Airbnb until you follow all the requirements. That can quickly affect your Airbnb, and you will lose guests for a period of time. Essentially, this means that your rental property is not making money, but you are still left to pay the bills and fines.

Risk of Vacancy

One of the first factors you should think of before opening an Airbnb is that you may not have tenants constantly. Even if you live in a high tourism area, you can still find your Airbnb vacant for a month or two. You may even have tenants who cancel on you at the last minute, which means you lose the money you were counting on, or you have to issue them a refund.

Most people follow the 24-hour rule. If the tenant alerts you that they need to cancel 24 hours before their check-in time, they are free of any fees. However, if they do not cancel and do not show up, then you will continue to charge their card. When this happens, expect them or their credit card company to contact you, as they will try to get out of the charges. You will need proof that they did not notify you of their cancellation, and need to ensure your policy is in place and that they already know about it.

There are several ways to protect yourself from the risk of vacancy, especially when it comes to quieter tourist seasons. Firstly, you want to thoroughly research the location for your Airbnb. Secondly, you want to think about lowering prices, or doing something special that will make guests choose your Airbnb over another one in the area, especially during low-tourist seasons. Thirdly, you want to always make sure that you have enough cash flow to get you through the tougher months. There are a number of Airbnb profitability calculators to help you understand occupancy rates, capital rates, and cash returns for your location.

Chapter 3: Location Research

When you are performing your research, you may want to look at all the factors you can think of. You will start your research by looking at the best locations, and then find yourself looking at establishing house rules, insurance, and hidden expenses. If you do not organize your research from the start, you will become overwhelmed. This can lead you to think negatively about owning an Airbnb. You might start to feel that you will not succeed because the process is too long, or that you can't afford it.

The first step you want to take when you start to feel overwhelmed is to take a step back. Leave your research for a period of time. It won't go anywhere, and you can return to your computer as soon as you start feeling better. The next step to follow is to take your research into smaller steps. You don't need to learn everything all at once. When people have an idea to invest in property, they want to jump on the bandwagon and start making money as fast as possible. One of the most common mistakes for investing beginners is thinking that they will make money quickly. In reality, it is a slow journey, but once you open your Airbnb, you will quickly notice the benefit, see your bank account grow, and realize that going slowly is much better than jumping into investing.

If you have never spent much time researching, this can feel like an overwhelming task. Fortunately, the research phase is easier than it looks. However, it does take a lot of time, and you may need to spend some money for copies of information and other research fees.

The general research process is basic. You will be following these steps as a guide when you start focusing on your research:

1. Identify your topic.
2. Look for background information in your area and on Airbnbs in general.
3. Start a basic online search for a general idea of your location and tourist information. Look to see what other Airbnbs are in your area.
4. Go to the library, city, county, and state offices to look for statistics.
5. Evaluate all of your research.

Take time to think about your specific research steps. In the space provided, write information on each step to give you a start on your research process.

1. _____
2. _____
3. _____
4. _____
5. _____

Market Research

One of the biggest types of research you will focus on when looking for your location is market research. This looks specifically at statistics and other factors to help you determine the best location for your Airbnb. Because this is a specific type of research, you will need to go beyond Google or Yahoo! for your research. However, these search engines are a great place to start. You will want to go to your city offices to see if there are any statistics on Airbnbs and also gather tourism information. This can lead you to narrow down the best locations for your Airbnb.

Part of market research is looking at other prices of Airbnbs and rental properties people can temporarily stay at. You will want to get an average price and be in the range of this, but you don't want the most expensive Airbnb, especially when you are first starting out. Furthermore, you can't set your price too low such that you struggle to pay bills and save money for repairs.

With market research, you want to understand the difference between primary and secondary research. Primary research is the information that is gotten firsthand. For example, statistics from surveys and reports. Secondary information is information written about previously. For example, if someone writes an article about tourism in your area based on the survey reports, the article is secondary research. The main research you want to pay attention to is the firsthand information. While secondary research can help you, primary research is mainly facts that you can use to choose your best location.

AirDNA

One of the main tools you will use to help you focus on market research is AirDNA. AirDNA will give you information that you will not find anywhere else. The data collected and placed into AirDNA comes from the Airbnb website. AirDNA can feel overwhelming at first, but it is essential that you look into this database. This is a tool that you want to use often, as it will help you grow as a host. You will understand more about the Airbnb world, what your guests want, how to manage your investments, guests, staff, and make the right decisions. AirDNA helps you understand that your business will grow, but this will take time.

Identify Your Competition

Through your research, you will need to identify your competition. You will do this through your primary and secondary market research. You can find Airbnbs in your area through doing online research, the Airbnb website, and the statistics and reports of your local governmental offices.

It is important to realize the rate of growth when it comes to the Airbnb community. There are hundreds of new locations added to the Airbnb website daily. You want to keep up with your competition. You don't want to focus on your competition during your beginning research phase. You want to pay attention to all the new Airbnbs in your area, what the current prices are, and what services they offer. People are constantly changing their Airbnb, and it is important that you keep up with your competition.

Understanding Listings

Another part of your market research is making sure you understand the listings. You can learn a lot about running your Airbnb by looking at the current listings in your area and surrounding areas. For example, if you are opening an Airbnb in Florida, you will want to start by looking at a 25-mile radius from your possible location. You will then expand to 50 miles and even look into neighboring states.

There are four main parts of a listing (What factors determine how my listing appears in the search results?, n.d.):

- **Price.** The prices of other Airbnbs in your area will become the deciding factor of your Airbnb price. You might not want yours to be the lowest price, but you will want to be cheaper than most, especially in the beginning. You will need to create a budget to ensure that you can make the bills and still have

capital every month, but you do not want to be the most expensive Airbnb.
- **New listing.** The Airbnb website lists the newest listing first when they show up in searches. The website is available to help you establish your business. They will use algorithms to ensure your listing is noticed when people are searching for accommodation in your area.
- **Reviews.** Reviews are incredibly important on the Airbnb website and for your business. The more reviews you have, the more people will notice your Airbnb. You should highly consider not only asking people to leave reviews, but also giving them a coupon for a local business or a discount for their next stay for leaving a positive review.
- **Superhost.** Once you pass certain requirements, the Airbnb website lists you as a superhost. This is a high honor, and one that people look for when they are searching for a place to stay on their vacation.

These listing factors are important for you to notice in your research and remember throughout your process. Take a moment to highlight or write this information down. Have it available when you need a reminder, especially when you are starting to create your advertisements and listing your Airbnb on the website.

Best and Worst U.S. Cities for Airbnb

The housing market in your area can make or break the chance of establishing an Airbnb. For instance, there are many states where purchasing a home is too expensive. This causes people to rent instead of buy. Of course, you can always make a deal with your landlord to get them on the same page with your Airbnb idea.

However, if you are serious about becoming an Airbnb host and willing to go anywhere in the world to make this happen, then you will want to choose one of the best locations for Airbnb rentals (Saldana, 2019).

Best Places for One- and Two-Bedroom Properties

- **Nashville, Tennessee.** Monthly rent is $1,380 and arbitrage potential is $1,663.
- **Des Moines, Iowa.** Monthly rent is $810 and arbitrage potential is $1,190. (One bedroom properties only.)
- **Honolulu, Hawaii.** Monthly rent is $1,700 and arbitrage potential is $1,746.
- **Boston, Massachusetts.** Monthly rent is $2,400 and arbitrage potential is $1,520.
- **Detroit, Michigan.** Monthly rent is $610 and arbitrage potential is $1,273.
- **Corpus Christi, Texas.** Monthly rent is $1,070 and arbitrage potential is $1,620. (Two bedroom properties only.)

Worst Places for One Bedroom Properties

- **San Francisco, California.** Monthly rent is $3,700 and arbitrage potential is -$455.

- **New York, New York.** Monthly rent is $2,850 and arbitrage potential is -$302.
- **Laredo, Texas.** Monthly rent is $830 and arbitrage potential is -$285.
- **Oakland, California.** Monthly rent is $2,270 and arbitrage potential is -$295.
- **San Jose, California.** Monthly rent is $2,850 and arbitrage potential is -$412.

Worst Place for Two Bedroom Properties.

- **Irving, Texas.** Monthly rent is $1,490 and arbitrage potential is -$399.
- **Chandler, Arizona.** Monthly rent is $1,440 and arbitrage potential is -$263.
- **Scottsdale, Arizona.** Monthly rent is $2,080 and arbitrage potential is -$403.
- **Oakland, California.** Monthly rent is $2,720 and arbitrage potential is -$89.
- **Laredo, Texas.** Monthly rent is $940 and arbitrage potential is -$230.

Chapter 4: Hidden Expenses

There are more expenses than meets the eye when it comes to your Airbnb rentals. No matter how much research you do, new expenses will pop up from time to time. These expenses will catch you off-guard and leave you frustrated. You might have to dig deep into your account to pay for certain repairs — even ones that insurance will help pay for. There are also expenses that happen and need to be fixed immediately, so you can continue renting your space. When it comes to these expenses, insurance will not send you money to fix anything quickly. You will need to pull from your cash flow and then place the insurance check into your account when you receive it.

Thinking of All Your Expenses

It is nearly impossible to think of all your expenses, especially if this is the first investment you will make. Thinking of expenses is easy if you are a homeowner.

You understand that some expenses will surprise you. You will automatically think of maintenance, utility bills, city fees for garbage and sewer systems, and taxes. However, many investors do not own their homes. They may live in their Airbnb, or they might live in an apartment and try to find a way to plant their feet in an investment career. No matter what your story here, here are some of the major expenses to take into consideration.

Keys

You will always need access into your Airbnb. At the same time, you want to allow your tenants to feel secure in the rental, and this means they need to lock themselves in their area without worry about anyone, including you, coming in at any moment. This means that you will want to have different locks on doors, whether you rent out rooms or a whole house. You will want separate locks for the areas that are inaccessible to your tenants, such as a basement, attic, and office. This can leave you with a lot of keys. While three different keys may seem manageable, if you have several Airbnbs, you will want to think about a master key. This is a key that will get you into any locked room. You are the only person having the master key, while your tenants have keys strictly for their areas. Locks and keys can both be keyed to a specific master key. All you need to do is take everything to your local locksmith, and they will help you with the rest.

Along with keys, a lockbox is a necessity. For example, if you have multiple Airbnbs and staff that need access to the master key, you can place a master key in a lockbox and give your staff the code to get into the lockbox. This keeps you from making several master keys, and, at the same time, eases the fear of one key getting lost, or someone taking a master key with them.

Furnishing Your Airbnb

People don't want to stay at an Airbnb with furniture that doesn't match. While this might not bother you as it is part of your budget, people will remember how the place looked. If you have a green recliner that is a bit stained, a brown sofa, and black chairs, people will feel your Airbnb is a bit of an eyesore. Think about what you see when you walk into hotels or rentals you stay in. The furniture that matches gives the place a homey feel and makes people believe that the host cares about how the Airbnb looks.

This means, especially if you are turning your home into an Airbnb, that you may need to buy new furniture. This can put a big dent into your budget, but you will quickly make the money back if your tenants are happy. Some of your best advertising is happy tenants because they will tell their friends besides leaving you a positive review.

Another factor to think of when furnishing is to give your tenants space. Don't clutter the space with too many chairs, a bed that is too big for a room, tables, desk, bookcase, and everything else. Think of what your tenants will absolutely need. You can also research other Airbnbs. Maybe you will spend a night at several Airbnbs to get an idea for your design. You may research pictures on Google, or go to online forums where people share their experiences.

Bills and Taxes

People expect bills and taxes when it comes to their rental, but they don't often think about all the bills. For instance, you will naturally think of the utility bill, cable, and Internet. But, you might not consider fees when people use credit cards to pay. Most hosts have everything set up online, so the tenant can pay for their space. The payment system will charge their card, and you will receive a smaller amount of money than what the room initially cost. For example, if you set the price of the room at $200 a night, you may only receive $190 because the charging system and credit card company took the $10 as their fee for processing the payment. Look into your payment system to see what type of processing fees they charge. Include this fee into the rental. You don't need to inform people of the fee; you can simply add it into the cost of the Airbnb. If you include too many fees and list them all for the tenant to see, they may turn down your Airbnb because they feel you include too many fees. Even if you charge these fees because they are charged to you, tenants don't necessarily understand these fees.

Cleaning Services

Will you clean your Airbnb every day to make sure that it looks nice and your tenants are happy? Are you going to spend time cleaning their room and making the bed like hotels do on a daily basis? Chances are, you are busy trying to manage more than one rental, or other parts of your Airbnb. This means you will need to hire someone to do the cleaning. Even if you have a small space, this can still take one person a few hours to clean. Therefore, you need to factor in cleaning supplies, their pay, and any type of benefits you give to your employees. Your employees are more likely to stay if they feel appreciated and are paid well. Benefits, starting pay, pay raises, and insurance are all important factors to consider when hiring staff. In most states, you have to have some type of insurance to hire staff.

Hidden Structural Problems

You purchased a newer home in a location with a lot of tourists throughout the year. You felt this location was the best option for your new Airbnb. Unfortunately, two months into owning the place, contractors noticed some structural damage. As they show you the foundation damage, you ask them how this could happen as the home is only five years old. They tell you that the previous contractors built the home quickly and poorly. They also inform you that it needs to be repaired or you won't pass your inspection. This means you can't open your Airbnb on time.

The best way to overcome hidden structural problems is through a savings account. Have money set aside that you constantly deposit into for repairs. Of course, there is always the option of taking out any loan for the larger repairs, but a loan shouldn't be the first place you go to when there is a structural problem. At the same time, you never want your savings for repairs to drop too low.

Other hidden expenses can happen because of your guests. Most Airbnb rentals are homes. Your guests have access to the home, which means that you do not enter it, unless for emergencies or given permission by your guests, or until they leave. It is your guests' right to have their privacy. The biggest problems occur when your tenant leaves early without informing you, or causes damage. For example, you think that an insurance agent is staying in your Airbnb, but when you walk into the home the day after they are scheduled to leave, you find walls damaged, water running, and a flood on your kitchen floor. The estimated damage from everything is $25,000. While you can contact the tenant and demand they pay for the damages, it is more likely that you will need to take them to court. In this case, you will need to add court costs and other legal fees. Plus, it will take time for you to get to court and receive the money, providing you win. This doesn't help your biggest problem – you need to make the repairs as quickly as possible. Remember, even insurance companies can take time before issuing you their check. On top of that, they might not even cover all the repairs.

Chapter 5: Striking an Agreement with the Landlord

If you do not own your home or the space for your Airbnb, one of the most challenging steps is making an agreement with your landlord. This is a step that can cause a lot of emotions and anxiety, especially if you don't have a strong relationship with your landlord. However, there are also positives when talking to your landlord about establishing an Airbnb. For example, your landlord can think of questions that you didn't think about. If you are new to renting, your landlord may also give you some advice and tips to help you get started.

Always remember, there are a lot of concerns when it comes to establishing an Airbnb. You are not the only person that will have these concerns – your landlord will, too. The biggest difference is if you have worked through one of your concerns with research. If your landlord is just hearing of this idea, they might be a bit shocked and react quickly. If your landlord isn't sure about this situation, offer to sit them down and talk to them about your research and plan. Be open to any questions, concerns, and agreements they want to make. Furthermore, allow them time to process all the information.

Tips for Talking to Your Landlord

Before you talk to your landlord, you want a strong understanding of Airbnbs. You want to do thorough research, talk to other hosts, read through the Airbnb website, and analyze everything. When you know the details of Airbnb hosting, statistics, and understand your research, you can easily answer any questions that your landlord will have. On top of this, here are a few tips to help you talk to your landlord.

Make Your First Impression Great

Even if you have talked to your landlord before, make the first meeting about the possibility of an Airbnb a great impression. Start by talking about yourself and your goals. Let them get to know you as a person, but don't make the conversation strictly about you.

Discuss with them how you take care of your home, and how you plan to take care of any Airbnb you host.

Ask your landlord if they would like to view your home. Landlords can't walk into anyone's home, even if they own the property, as this is illegal. The only reason this is possible is if you let them inside, or there is an emergency. In some states, the police need to be on the grounds if there is an emergency. By inviting your landlord in, you are establishing a strong relationship.

Know Guidelines and Rules

As you are focusing on your research, pay attention to all the rules and regulations your city, county, and state set. Understand how contracts and leases will affect you, what rights you have, and what rights your tenants have. You should also be honest with your landlord. If you don't understand something, ask them. Don't act like you need to know everything. Know that you should have a good grasp on your research, but your landlord has hands-on experience, and this can be incredibly helpful to you.

Airbnb Community

Show your landlord the Airbnb website, and let them know this site is built on trust and respect. They want to help Airbnb hosts. Allow them time to look through the website on their own time. You can show them some of the most important pages, and point out valuable information.

How Do Your Neighbors Feel?

Before you meet with your landlord, set up a plan to talk to the neighbors or have support from your neighbors on hand. Show your landlord this information, and ask them what they think. Don't go into this conversation with the attitude that it is your way or no way. Let your landlord have as much say as they feel they need to, because this is a team effort.

Always Remain Calm and Understanding

You want to have the best attitude when you talk to your landlord about hosting an Airbnb. You want them to understand that you realize the risks, but still have a lot to learn. Your landlord might feel that you don't truly understand, because they manage rental properties. No matter how your landlord reacts to your request and information, the best option you have is to remain understanding and calm. If you feel your landlord is becoming disrespectful, have a plan of action to end the meeting. You can always request to meet with them at another time, after they have thought about everything you have said and looked through your information. Sometimes, people need some time to process information before they can think rationally.

Consider Their Position

One of the worst mistakes you can make is going to your landlord and acting like this is strictly a business meeting. You need to understand your landlord's position. Take a moment to think about how much you know about your landlord. Chances are, you know very little when it comes to your landlord's investments. Whether they own a lot of properties or not, allowing you to host an Airbnb is a big commitment for them. Even if they take a backseat and don't do much of the work, they still need to be involved and considered, and this includes their emotions and opinions on your idea.

Tips for Handling the Agreement

Unless your landlord is impressed and excited about the Airbnb opportunity, coming to an agreement will take a while. You need to show patience and understanding throughout the process. You don't want to give up hope, even if it is a couple of months without communication from your landlord. Furthermore, don't be afraid to send them a message if you haven't heard from them in a while. Don't make them feel overwhelmed by contacting them too often.

Be Willing to Negotiate

You will need to negotiate when it comes to the agreement. You may come with a great plan and have nearly perfect terms, but your landlord has a lot of other terms and conditions that don't match up with yours. Take a deep breath and realize that this is part of the negotiation.

Control Your Emotions

It's easy to allow your emotions to take control when you are in an intense situation. Even if you and your landlord believe an Airbnb is a great idea, coming to an agreement can be challenging. You might feel attacked over your terms and conditions. You might also feel that your landlord is trying to take complete control over the situation, or you don't agree with all of your landlord's terms, but they seem to be pushing them onto you. Some people struggle with negotiations because it is a new territory. All of these factors can make your emotions boil over and take control of the situation. When this happens, you are not going to think clearly. Do your best to control your emotions so that you can think rationally when coming to an agreement.

How Would You React?

After reading through all of these tips, I want you to imagine meeting and coming to an agreement with your landlord. Psychologically, visualizing a positive process helps people feel more confident when they take the next step. The more you visualize coming to an agreement, the less anxious you will feel and the more you will be in control.

Take a moment to think about how you will ask your landlord to meet with you to discuss Airbnb hosting and the agreement process. Write your visualization down below:

Chapter 6: Furnished vs. Unfurnished Units

To furnish or not furnish your Airbnb? This is one of the biggest questions new hosts have when it comes to their rental. The answer most people will give is that you should always furnish your Airbnb, as this keeps your tenants happy. However, there are also tenants who prefer to furnish the place themselves, especially if they plan on staying there for a few months or so.

Some hosts discovered the best way to handle this situation is to have a couple of properties that are furnished, and a couple that are unfurnished. Unfortunately, this is not an option for everyone, especially a new host who doesn't have the means or finances to support more than one Airbnb. To help you make the decision, let's look at both types of Airbnbs.

Furnished

If you decide to furnish your Airbnb, you want to take your time on it. This is an important step. In fact, some people say it is as important as finding the perfect location. You need to ensure that you take your time to find the best furniture. Don't simply go to one store and choose your furniture there. You want to look around and think about how each piece will fit nicely in the place. It might help you to take pictures of the walls, floors, and lights to make sure the furniture you pick will fit in perfectly with the home.

You need to think more than how the furniture will look. You also need to think about the function of the furniture. How are your guests going to use the furniture? Are you going to allow pets in the Airbnb? If so, what factors do you need to take into consideration so that your furniture does not get ruined?

If you do decide on furniture, here is a list that most hosts include in their rental unit:

- Dining room – table and chairs
- Living room – couch, end table, television (optional), lamps
- Kitchen – refrigerator, stove, oven, toaster, and microwave

- Bedroom – bed frame, mattress, bedding, dresser, end table (optional), desk (optional)
- Bathroom – linens and shower curtains

You can also decorate your Airbnb with wallpaper, art, and other types of decorations to give the place a home-like atmosphere.

After you have all the essential furniture, it is time to think about curtains, blinds, and other coverings for the windows. You want to turn on the lights and consider adding any type of lighting. While your tenants can bring their own lamps, if they are travelers, they won't come with much, and won't want to spend money on something they can't travel with. Therefore, it is always a good idea to have extra lighting. Your tenants will use the amount of lighting they are comfortable with.

Function of the Furniture

When you think of the function, you want to focus on specific tenants. Even though you will meet a variety of people from different backgrounds, it is important to find a target tenant when picking out furniture. You can think of anyone you want to, such as a couple on their honeymoon or an insurance agent who is traveling for business. Whoever you choose, you will think about what type of furniture they will need during their stay. For example, if you are thinking about an insurance agent, you will want to invest in a desk so they have space to work.

Take a moment to think about your target tenant. Write down why your tenant is at your Airbnb, and what type of furnishings they will need for a pleasant experience:

_____
_____
_____
_____
_____
_____
_____
_____
_____

Decorating

When it comes to decorating, it is important to focus on themes and certain colors. You want everything to fit together, yet you don't want to overwhelm your guests with the same few colors. If you plan on decorating, here are a few tips to consider:

- **Think about bed space.** People like to travel in groups when they are on vacation, or it might be a whole family. The more space you have for beds, the easier it will be to find guests. Think of getting a couch that can pull out into a bed, or a futon in a spare room, such as an office.
- **Have plenty of electrical outlets.** One of the most annoying factors guests talk about is that the Airbnb didn't have enough outlets. While you may need to call in an electrician, you want to make sure there are plenty of outlets for everyone's devices and other chargeable items.
- **Colors.** You want the colors to appeal to as many people as possible. Use neutral colors, and don't focus on colors that people might feel are too bright. You also want to stay away from colors that are too dark.
- **Mirrors.** There are some people that don't mind mirrors in their homes, and other people who would rather stay away from mirrors. You want to be careful of any mirrors in your Airbnb. Take a moment to think of the best

places for a mirror, such as the bedroom, bathroom, and near the front door. Don't place mirrors randomly around the home.

Unfurnished

The biggest benefit to having an unfurnished Airbnb is that you don't need to think about the furniture and decorating. However, you are more likely to make people interested in your Airbnb if it has some type of appeal. Therefore, you may want to place a few accent pieces around the home, as this will give people the idea that this unfurnished place can become their home for a while.

One factor to consider before you decide on an unfurnished Airbnb is if people will walk away from your place because there is no furniture. While some people may only stay for a couple of nights, they will still want a place to sleep, work, and something to do, such as watching television or receiving WiFi so that they can use their laptops.

You also want to think of the price. People will pay more money for a furnished space because they understand that they are paying to use the furniture and other services. If you do not furnish the place, you will want to make sure you get the average price of Airbnbs in your area that are not furnished. It should not be the same price as furnished Airbnbs.

Chapter 7: Understanding the Neighbors

Before you go too far in your Airbnb planning, you want to look into your surroundings and talk to your neighbors. When I discuss looking into your surroundings, I am talking about the area closest to you. For example, are there businesses in your surrounding area or is it a residential area? Is there space for your guests to hang up their laundry or allow their children to run around and play in the front yard? By checking out your surroundings, you can think of several benefits to pull your guests in to your Airbnb.

Part of checking your surroundings is your neighbors. In fact, your neighbors can influence your guest's experience at the Airbnb. For instance, if you have a neighbor that is trying to shut your Airbnb down because they don't like the idea of strangers in the neighborhood, they might cause problems with your guests and give them an unpleasant experience.

One of the keys to handling your neighbors when establishing an Airbnb is to talk to them about this.

First, you want to make sure that you don't need to get your neighbors to agree to your Airbnb. Some city regulations will ask you to get your neighbors to sign a form stating that they agree to the Airbnb in their neighborhood. If this is the case in one area, you can always look into another area if you can't convince a neighbor to agree to an Airbnb. However, if you have found the perfect spot, you already own the property, or have an agreement with your landlord, then you may want to try to convince your neighbors that your Airbnb will not cause problems.

Tips When Talking to Your Neighbors

Understand Your Neighbors

One of the best tips you will receive is to understand your neighbors. While you don't need to talk to them exactly like you did with your landlord, it is important you do request to discuss any concerns or questions they have. A lot of people don't like change, especially when it threatens their home. Psychologically, people have a need to feel secure in their homes. When you bring in strangers, this threatens their security. It doesn't mean that they believe everyone who rents from you will cause problems or destroy property. They don't believe that everyone is a bad person. However, they do realize that the potential for problems is greater. Naturally, we live in a society where there is fear when it comes to the unknown, and this includes people. If they don't know the person, they might be skeptical of them.

You want to be as patient with your neighbors as you are with your landlord. You need to remember that this is a new topic for them, whereas you have thought about it for months, completed research, and became comfortable with the idea. They need to become comfortable with the idea as well, and this takes time.

Ask Your Neighbors to Meet with You

Tell your neighbors that you are thinking of opening an Airbnb and want them to be informed of the process. Ask them to take time to sit down with you, where they can ask you any questions and speak their concerns. Give them some information from your research to get them used to the idea. While they might not take the time to read it, they will appreciate the fact that you went out of your way to give them the information. Quickly talking to them will allow you to read their body language, or get a sense of how they feel about the idea through their tone of voice. For example, if they seem interested in the idea, they will want to sit down and talk to you. If they are unsure, they might be hesitant to talk to you. People don't want to do something where they feel like they are wasting their time. Therefore, if they don't want an Airbnb in the neighborhood, they won't care to meet with you.

Have a Neighborhood Meeting

The type of neighborhood will depend on if you decide to invite all your neighbors to a neighborhood meeting or not. In this meeting, you will discuss the Airbnb community. You can talk about the brief history, discuss positive stories, and show them the Airbnb website. Tell them that the community wants to help the Airbnb become a pleasant experience for everyone. Take time to discuss any concerns that your neighbors have and answer any questions. Furthermore, you will want to talk about your research and give them benefits to how the Airbnb can help the community.

Talk About Safety

Remember, one of the biggest reasons your neighbor may be hesitant about an Airbnb is because they feel it is a threat to their home and community. Tell them about the safety procedures and what you are doing to make sure that your Airbnb and the community remains safe. Discuss any policies that you are willing to, and ask them for input. People naturally feel more comfortable about an idea when they feel a part of it. This doesn't mean that they will become your partners. It means that you understand they are part of the neighborhood, and have a right to make sure their homes and families are safe. Plus, they might think of situations that you didn't.

Offer Notice of Guests

Offer to keep your neighbors informed of any new guests. While they don't need to know any information about these guests, you can call them or email them to say that a family of five will be staying at the Airbnb for a couple of weeks starting on this date. Of course, you always need to follow any confidentiality procedures set up by the Airbnb community and yourself. Keeping your neighbors informed will allow them to know what is going on and feel safer. They can also ask you questions, such as how this will affect street parking if there are a lot of people at once.

Be Honest About Claims

You may not want to tell them, but it is important that your neighbors understand that they can file a claim if someone throws a party, or they feel the Airbnb is causing too many problems within the community. They can file claims with the city police department or they can go online to the Airbnb website and fill out a form. You can even take this time to talk to your neighbors about a procedure. For example, they should call you about any problem or concern before they go ahead and file a claim. As part of the Airbnb community, you want everyone to be comfortable and have a good experience, including your neighbors.

Visualization Exercise

Talking to your neighbors about your Airbnb can cause anxiety. You might want to ignore this step because you are unsure of what your neighbors will say, or how they will feel. This would be a mistake. You want to make sure you connect with your neighbors and keep them informed, especially if they request it.

To help you overcome any nerves you may have with talking to your neighbors, I want you to take a moment to visualize hosting a meeting to discuss turning your unit into an Airbnb. You can go through the process of giving a short history, talking about good and bad stories, and then coming up with a procedure for any problems. Write down your visualization, tips, or ideas you have below. This will help you become more comfortable with the idea of talking to your neighbors.

Chapter 8: Making the Unit Airbnb Ready

There is a lot of preparation that goes into preparing your home to become an Airbnb. It is important that you take your time with this process. You will make more mistakes or forget a step when you are rushing. You want everything to be as perfect as possible from the time you open your Airbnb for its first guest. Of course, you always want to realize that you will learn as you go through your first few guests, or even your first 20. In fact, it means that you are always willing to grow as an Airbnb host.

Steps and Tips to Prepare Your Home

There are several steps you should follow when it comes to making your unit Airbnbready. However, you won't follow all these steps at once. You will start once you decide to go with the idea and you will finish when you are ready for your first guests.

1. *Keep Your Eyes Open for Safety*

You want to walk around your whole house and notice anything that might not be safe for your guests. For example, are there cracks in your foundation, or is there a cracked window in the basement? Are there exposed wires, or do you have an outlet that sparks when you plug a cord into it? All these questions are something you should focus on when you are walking around your home. You will want to fix any loose hand railings, and make sure that your guests have one of the safest Airbnb rental units available. While this will cost money, you will quickly notice the benefits through the happiness and comfort of your guests.

You will also want to ensure that any smoke alarms, security alarms, and carbon monoxide detectors are working correctly. Make sure they have not expired and that you follow your city or state laws when it comes to changing these devices out. It is always a great idea to have a first aid kit, and to make sure the fire extinguisher works correctly.

Other factors to consider are leaving your contact information available for your guests at the front door, or by the landline. Even though people use their cellphones, it is still a good idea to install a landline for safety reasons.

2. *Clean Before Photographs*

One of the steps you will complete before listing your Airbnb is taking great photographs. If you don't feel you can take professions pictures, then you can always hire a professional photographer. But, no matter who takes the pictures, one of the biggest steps you want to accomplish is cleaning. Make sure that all your decorations and furniture is in place, and then give the Airbnb a deep cleaning. If you don't feel you can clean well enough, hire a cleaning person. However, you want to make sure that nothing is out of place and everything looks practically perfect before anyone snaps pictures.

It is also important to think about doing a deep clean before any new guest comes into your Airbnb. One factor about having great photos in your listing is that people are going to expect the Airbnb to look at the pictures. If they walk into a mess or a partially-made bed, they are going to feel like they picked the wrong Airbnb.

3. Don't Have Anything Out That You Don't Want Your Guests to Touch

While you will want to have decor, you don't want to leave your valuables around for your guests to touch or worse – steal. If this is your home, you stay there, or if you are there part-time, you want to lock away any of your valuables. This may mean that your guests do not have access to the basement, attic, or your bedroom. Whatever the case is, you want to make sure that everything you don't want them to see is secure before you take pictures.

4. Stop Your Mail

If you allow Airbnb guests in your home when you are on vacation, a business trip, or gone, you'll want to make sure that you stop your mail. You need to head to your post office to fill out a form, asking them to hold your mail for a specific time period. This ensures that your guests won't receive your mail, your mail won't be lost, or no one will get curious to open your mail. You always need to take the right steps for safety reasons.

5. Provide a Check-In for When You Are Not There

Unless you can confide in a friend or ensure you can be at your Airbnb, you want to provide a way for your guests to check in and receive their keys without anyone there. For example, you may send the keys in the mail, or leave them in a lockbox with instructions once they get there.

While providing self-check-in and -check-out is fine, and many Airbnb hosts do this, it always gives you an extra boost of hospitality to meet your guests. You might feel this helps ease your mind, too, as you have met your guests, and can gain a sense of trust through meeting them.

6. Provide Brochures and Menus

Most people who stay at your Airbnb are new to the area. They won't know what type of restaurants your city has, or what activities there are for them. Provide this information near your check-out area, or place it somewhere they can see. Have a few copies of each, just in case they want to take the information with them, or if they get lost, or ruined.

It is always a nice touch to give your guests something that helps them remember your Airbnb. For example, talk to your local museum or zoo to see if you can create an agreement for your guests. If they stay at your Airbnb, they receive a discount for 25% off admission or something from the business' gift shop. Most businesses are happy to work something out with an Airbnb, as this gives them more business.

7. *Equip Your Airbnb for Its Guests*

When it comes to preparing your home for Airbnb renting, you want to make sure you have everything accounted for. It is easy for people who own the home to run out and purchase an item they need, such as new bedding or toaster, but not as easy for your guests. You need to remember that they are guests, and this means that everything should be accounted for. While you want to include basic foods, such as butter, salt, and seasonings, many hosts don't worry about staking up the kitchen, as people have different tastes. Plus, if your guests are new to the area, they will want to experience the restaurants and food from your culture. This is why it is always a great idea to leave menus and a phone book for them.

Some of the items to ensure your Airbnb has for its guests are (Fishman, n.d.):

- First-aid kit
- Cleaning supplies
- Soap (hand soap, dishwashing liquid, laundry detergent, carpet cleaning, etc.)
- Garbage bags
- Empty the garbage and recycling bins
- Fans
- Fire extinguisher
- Basic toiletries
- Potholders
- Microwave
- Toaster
- Ironing board
- Iron
- Clean linens
- Extra bedding
- Protectors for mattress and pillows
- Light bulbs
- Any remotes for devices

There are also features that you can add to make your guests' experience as great as possible. Some of these features may make their way into your guests' suitcase. In this case, you want to look into having your logo or name on the item. This is not so you can call your guest to get the items back; it is a form of advertising. This also means you won't want to spend a lot of money on these items. For example, if you leave any DVDs for your guests to watch, look at garage sales or the sale bins at stores.

- DVDs
- Card games
- Basic food, such as milk, cereal, coffee, snacks
- Hair dryer
- Items that they can take with them, such as bottles of wine or local delicacies.

Visualization Exercise

Take a moment to think of how you would set up your Airbnb. How will you make your place stand out from the rest of the competition, especially in a larger area? What kinds of gifts will you set out for your guests? What items will you ensure your guests have, to make their experience memorable? Write down some ideas, your list of items, or even a detailed plan that you imagine.

Chapter 9: What About Insurance?

When it comes to insurance, no one is going to force you to get any type of insurance. It is similar to rental or home insurance; it is a great idea to have, but it is up to you. Before you skip the insurance part, I want you to take a minute to think about how insurance can help you in a bind, or when something bad happens. For example, one of your guests is walking down the stairs when they slip and fall, breaking their ankle. Without insurance, the guest can sue you for not making the stairs safer, for instance, providing non-slip protection for removing the carpet. What about if there is a fire, or someone damages your property? Insurance can help you in these times. Insurance not only protects you, but your guests, too.

Before you jump into finding the best insurance for you and your Airbnb, you need to know the laws within your state. There are some U.S. states that have certain regulations to determine if you will qualify for Airbnb insurance, renter's insurance, or any other type of insurance. No matter what type of insurance you feel is best for you, it is important to understand everything about your insurance. Meet with a local insurance agent, as they can help you through this process. You always want to ensure that your insurance is in place and valid before you allow guests into your Airbnb.

Airbnb Insurance

There are two forms of coverage under the Airbnb insurance. The first is Host Guarantee, and the second is Host Protection Insurance. Both of these policies are important to look at and understand before you decide to open your Airbnb.

Airbnb insurance policies cover up to $1 million in protection for every situation where you need to file an insurance claim. For example, if a storm comes and a tree falls on your Airbnb, you are covered for up to $1 million in damages. If your guest falls and hurts themselves on a weak step, they cannot sue you. Instead, your insurance will pay your guests' medical bills and any settlement for their injury. This doesn't mean that you should ignore potentially hazardous conditions in your Airbnb. There is always a chance that insurance will refuse to cover the situation because you did not take the necessary precautions to fix the step or cut down the tree. Never assume that your insurance will cover any situation.

Host Protection Insurance

The Airbnb Host Protection Insurance will cover situations when a guest makes a claim against you. For example, if your guest accidentally hurts someone on your property, themselves, or damages someone else's property, your Host Protection Insurance will cover this claim. Host Protection Insurance is great to have, because it will cover your property and any vehicles listed on the Airbnb website.

There are situations that are not covered under Host Protection Insurance. For example, if your guest gets into a physical fight with someone on your property, this is not covered. The insurance will not cover damage done during a party because they don't cover people who are intoxicated. They will not cover any type of mold that is found in your home. All of these situations you will have to deal with out of pocket, or add another type of insurance policy to your Airbnb.

Host Guarantee

The Host Guarantee will cover a lot of situations the Host Protection Insurance does not. Host Guarantee covers up to $1 million, but it is not considered an insurance policy like Host Protection Insurance. Because of this, there are certain steps you need to follow before you can claim a situation under your Host Guarantee protection.

You need to complete the whole claim process within 30 days. This means that you have to come to an agreement with the guest responsible for the situation. For example, if the guest threw a party and damaged your home and some furniture, you will ask them to pay for the damages. If they refuse, you need to notify the Airbnb of their refusal within 14 days of the guest's check-out date. By this point, you will need as much documentation, such as pictures and descriptions, of the damage as possible to give to the Airbnb. You also need to provide proof that you own the Airbnb and any of the furniture they damaged. If you do not complete this process within the timeframe, you will not receive any type of reimbursement. If you do meet the deadline, you will receive reimbursement that is equal to the cash value of your property. For instance, if your Airbnb's cash value is $25,000, then this is the amount you may receive to cover for damages. This is not always a guarantee. If the insurance agent feels that your property is not worth $25,000 because of physical depreciation, you will receive less. If your insurance doesn't cover the whole bill to repair the damage and the guest refuses to pay, you will need to come up with the rest. You can always try to sue the guest for damages, but this process takes time, and you will want to get your Airbnb back up and running quickly.

Renter's and Homeowner's Insurance

If you don't want to go the Airbnb insurance route, you can also look into renter's or homeowner's insurance. The type of insurance you receive will depend on if you own the property or not. However, you will want to make sure that your insurance company will cover damages caused by guests. There are some insurance companies that will not cover an

Airbnb. In this case, you will want to use Airbnb insurance coverage.

If you have renter's insurance, you want to read through your policy carefully, as there are often guidelines for subleasing. For example, some renter's insurance agencies will not cover guests who stay longer than three months. Some agencies refuse to offer coverage to people who make money through home-sharing. For instance, if you live in your home for six months and rent it out for six months, and receive $5,000 during this time period, most renter's insurance agencies will not cover you.

When it comes to renter's insurance, you will need to prove that you can home share. For example, you will send them your lease or a document from your landlord stating that they give you permission to manage an Airbnb.

Chapter 10: A How-to in Advertising

One of the strongest ways to get people into your door is through advertising. There are many ways to advertise, but one of your best options will be the Airbnb website. This is where you will handle communication with your guests, receive Airbnb insurance, and keep up-to-date on the Airbnb growth in the market.

If you feel that you don't have a creative gene for advertising, there is no need to worry. This chapter is to serve as a guide to help you overcome any anxieties about advertising and to create the best profile and listing to catch the interest of guests.

Personal Profile

One of the first steps you will need to take is creating your profile on Airbnb.

Profile Picture

You want to ensure your profile picture looks professional. It should show your face and give people the impression that you are approachable and friendly. People will look at your profile picture and most will judge your picture. If you are not smiling, they may skip you, because your picture doesn't give them a comforting feeling.

A Description About You

It is important that you realize your description is the first impression you will give your potential guest. You will introduce yourself, talk about your interests, and why you established your Airbnb. You don't want this description to become too long, yet you want to make it informative, fun, and engaging. It may help you to give the reader some fun facts about you.

What would you write in your description? You can start your description below or write some ideas that you would include in your description.

Taking Photographs

I already discussed the importance of cleaning up the place before you take photographs. You also want to make sure that you spend time organizing the rooms and getting them ready. You want the picture to look realistic as these pictures will help your guests decide if they should continue to look into your Airbnb or not. Therefore, have your theme set up, make your pictures colorful, and hire a professional photographer if you don't feel the pictures you take do your Airbnb justice.

While people want to make their pictures look perfect, you also need to make that your guests will walk into the same room they saw on Airbnb. If your guests see a clean and large apartment in the Airbnb site, and they check into an apartment that is crowded, is smelly, and is unkempt, they will not leave a positive review. They will feel like you betrayed them, and they will not trust you.

The photographs will become a part of your listing, so you want to ensure they match with the words you write. Other tips include:

- Make sure you have enough light in the room. This will bring out more color and make your pictures look professional.
- Take time to show your decor, especially the more unique pieces. For example, if you have a vase or rare piece of artwork, you will want to include this – as long as they will still be available for your guest to see in person.
- Don't forget about the outdoors. People want to see the inside and outside of the Airbnb, especially if they have children or pets. For instance, they may want a large yard that their children can play in.

- Don't forget about the corners. If you have a corner in the living with a unique item, take a picture. Corners can give the viewer a sense of how large the room truly is. When you take pictures of flat walls, they can't truly comprehend the size, and the room can look smaller.
- Take a lot of pictures. You may not use all the pictures, but people like pictures. They are interested and want to see as much as possible of their potential Airbnb. Don't give everything away, but give them enough that they are content and want to choose your place.

Writing Powerful Descriptions

Now that your profile is set and you have taken pictures, it is time to write the most powerful description possible. You will want to take time on your description and may have several drafts before you post the final one. However, you don't want to overthink writing your description, as this can cause you to miss important factors and feel overwhelmed with the process.

Always be honest in your description. Don't fluff up any details, as this will leave your guests disappointed. You want to give them a true experience of your Airbnb before they step foot into the unit.

You need to make your post engaging from the heading. You want to create a headline that will draw the viewers into your profile. You don't need to focus too much on this, as people are naturally drawn to certain words, such as: Amazing, great, lake view, etc. For example, "Amazing Lakeside Home" will gain their attention better than "Home for rent on the lake."

Write about the features that make your Airbnb stand out from everyone else. You want to make sure your description is detailed and gives the viewers the information they want to make the best decision. For example, how many people can stay in the Airbnb, how much bed space does the rental have, is there an attached garage, etc.? What type of additional services, such as laundry, do you have? Are these services for a one-time fee, or are they quarter machines? How do you access the home? Are there steps leading to a deck, or do you have a ramp?

Description Exercise

What type of description would you write? Even if you don't have an Airbnb yet, think of the one you want to establish. Because a description can become overwhelming to many people, you can focus on it in steps.

Step one: What one word adjective, such as "stylish" and "family-friendly", describes your home?
_____

Step two: How many bedrooms is your home?
_____

Step three: What special benefits and unique features does your home have? When thinking about this step, you want to think a bit outside of the box. For example, do you live near the ocean, a stadium, Disneyland, or another attraction? Be detailed in this step, as it will become most of your description.

_____
_____
_____
_____
_____

It might be helpful to write your features in a list form. For example, you will make a bulleted list of what the bedroom holds, kitchen, living room, etc. This can be part of your description, or be included on the bottom of your description.

Listing the Airbnb

Once you have your listing and photographs ready to activate on the Airbnb website, you need to follow these steps ("How do I activate my listing?", n.d.):

1. Make sure your listing is selected. You can write more than one listing and only activate the listings you want people to see.
2. Select "manage listing."
3. Select "edit" next to "listing status."
4. Once you receive the dropdown menu, click "listed."

5. Select "save", and your status will be updated in about an hour.

If you ever need to edit your listing, you will follow these steps and make whatever changes you need to after clicking "edit."

Chapter 11: Airbnb Ranking Tips

The main goal for all hosts is that they rank at the top of Airbnb's best listing. While the website does a lot to try to give the guests their best options, a search engine is not always the most reliable. There always seems to be great information that you miss through a regular search. Plus, if people limit their search too much, or they don't put in enough information, the search can easily miss your profile because it won't be selected.

Another reason you want to get on top of the listings is because people tend to look at the first few listings or first couple of pages and choose the best one. They don't feel that the listing near the end of the search will give them the best service. Psychologically, people assume that the best listings are at the top. Therefore, if you just uploaded your listing, you can easily miss out even if your listing is the best suited for the guest.

The determination for your ranking depends on 100 factors. The algorithm on the Airbnb site looks at such factors as reviews, price, if you are a superhost, if it's a new listing, the location, the guest's experience based on surveys, how quickly you respond to messages, and how many times people have clicked on your listing page (What factors determine how my listing appears in search results?, n.d.).

Ranking Tips

To help you reach the top, here are some of the best ranking tips for you to follow.

Use a Guest Welcome Book

The welcome book is a tool that can help your guests have the best experience once they step foot into your Airbnb. This is essential if you have an automated check-in service, as the welcome book will explain all the important information your guests need to know. It will also lessen the pressure of you needing to be right next to your phone when you have guests scheduled to arrive, as you might not have a designated time.

A welcome book can help maintain the flow of your Airbnb. You can list any information from procedures, such as the check-in and check-out processes, your methods of contact, what restaurants are close by, and what attractions are available. You can even include information that the guests can take home, or coloring books if they have brought children along. For example, some hosts ask their guests for a wish list of what they would like. A guest says they would like puzzles and games for the whole family to play instead of needing to focus on the televisions or their phones on a rainy day, or in the evening. The host takes out any puzzles and board games available in the home or purchases them. These are left near the welcome book for the guests to see when they arrive. As a host, you can decide if your guests keep these, or if they should stay for the next family.

Don't be Afraid to Over-Deliver

Some of the best hosts on the Airbnb site over-deliver. They don't make promises they can't keep. In fact, they will purposely under-promise so their guests are surprised and happy with the service nearly every time. A lot of hosts make the mistake of making promises they can't deliver. When this happens, your guests become frustrated because you did not give them what you promised. Promises are meant to be kept when you are running a business. Even if you know you can make a promise, it is sometimes best to keep it a secret and let your guests be surprised. Plus, when people are surprised, they feel special. You should always do what you can to ensure your guests feel special.

By keeping promises, giving your guests unexpected benefits, and setting a realistic impression of your Airbnb, you will reach 5-star reviews with nearly every stay.

Make Sure to Update Your Calendar Daily

Your schedule will determine where you sit in someone's search. The busier you are, the higher ranking you will receive. Your calendar doesn't automatically update, so you need to make sure this gets done every day. You might feel it is best to update your calendar every time you book another reservation, but some people can't spend their time doing this, especially if they have more than one

Airbnb. Updating your calendar will not only improve your ranking, but it will help you stay on top of your business. This will help you boost your rankings even more when you are given 5-star reviews!

Always Respond Within the Hour

Airbnb wants their hosts to respond within the hour. The algorithms pay attention to how quickly you respond to messages. When you let an hour pass by, even on the weekends when you don't want to work, you are harming your chances ranking at the top. Take the time to respond within one hour, no matter where you are or what you are doing.

Even if you decide to use the Instant Book, you always want to respond to your guests. An Instant Book is a tool that doesn't require you to approve your guests. It will automatically book the space and let other people know that your Airbnb is taken for that period of time (What is Instant Book?, n.d.). Guests have to make all of your requirements in order to book the space. It is up to you whether you want to use Instant Book or not. While it is convenient as it books the space without your response, many hosts feel more comfortable when they have communicated with the guests before approval.

Think Like a Guest

As you are writing your description or finding ways to communicate with your guests, think to yourself: What do my guests want? If I was a guest, what would I want? If you have trouble answering this question, think about spending time in an Airbnb. This will give you the mindset of a guest and help you notice what factors you are missing with your Airbnb.

Some of the main points to remember when thinking like a guest is they want a secure and comfortable place. They want information so they know where to eat, what attractions are in the area, and they want their host to deliver. For instance, if you tell your guests that there is extra bedding, then you make sure there is extra bedding. If you promise laundry facilities, then you need to ensure your machines are working.

You can also make each guest's experience a little different from the last one. Of course, you will change the experiences as you learn and grow as a host, but there is a difference between a business traveler and a digital nomad. A business traveler is in the area for their job. They might not spend a lot of time in the Airbnb, as they have meetings and responsibilities elsewhere. A digital nomad may spend most of their day in the Airbnb, as they need to work. However, they will spend the majority of their evenings checking out the sites and probably stay longer. For people that stay longer, you will need to have more communication with them. It is easy to allow a couple of days to pass by without speaking to your guests. However, you should not let more than a few days pass by without making sure that they are enjoying their stay. You will also need to check in with your long-term guests about any soap and other items they may need.

Cancel as Few Bookings as Possible

The number of cancellations you have, because of yourself or your guests, affects your ranking in the search engine. Aim to cancel as few bookings as possible, and you do have the right to refuse cancellations. It is important to note that, if you use Instant Book, a cancellation has to take place within

30 days to be free of charge. If a cancellation takes place after 30 days, you will be charged a cancellation fee (Airbnb Search Results: 10 Tips to Improve Your Ranking, 2019).

Don't Become Too Competitive with Pricing

It is important to know your market. You need to know the prices of other Airbnbs to set your price correctly. You want to be close to the average price, but you don't want to be the most expensive Airbnb in the area. You also don't want to undervalue your Airbnb, as this can lead to financial issues.

It is easy to get caught up in a price war with your competition. While you want to keep your competition at the back of your mind, you don't need to focus directly on them. At the end of the day, you need to do what is best for your Airbnb, yourself, and your guests.

You can always change the price of your Airbnb. A lot of hosts will raise their prices during the summer months, and lower them in the winter months. Some hosts will drop their prices if they don't have anyone booked over the next coming weeks as a special sale to try to draw people in. It is a good idea to change your prices now and then as this will keep people coming back to your page, making you rank a little higher on the Airbnb site.

Have Guests Add Your Listing to their Wishlists

When a guest likes the Airbnb they stayed at, they can add it to their wishlist on the site. This allows other people to see some of their favorite properties and look into them if they are going to the same location. When guests add your location to their wishlist, you automatically rank higher than hosts that are not on anyone's wishlist, as this is another factor the Airbnb algorithms pay attention to.

You can ask your guests to add you to their wishlist and give you a rating. You can do this during the checkout process by reminding them, or sending them correspondence after they have checked out, thanking them for their stay, and welcoming them back anytime.

Chapter 12: Managing Your Airbnb

By now, you have a pretty good handle on how you will start up your Airbnb. You understand that you need to take your time with the research process, you have to set up an account with Airbnb website, establish your rules and guidelines, and how to receive a top ranking. While all these factors are important, one of the most important steps in your Airbnb journey is managing your Airbnb.

Automating the Check-In Process and Tools

Making your check-in process automated is something that is completely up to you. Some hosts rent out a room in their home, so they are there daily. Other hosts will rent out their home when they leave, meaning they will not be there when their guests arrive. While you can hire someone to help manage your Airbnb when you aren't there, you can also take the automated route. However, you will always want someone to check on your Airbnb, clean it, and make sure the guests didn't damage property.

Automated Check-In

Many hosts use electronic keys as all they need to do is give their guests the code. Then, once the guest leaves your Airbnb, you can change the code. This eliminates the need to worry about making sure guests give you all their keys, and they didn't make copies. Even if keys have a "do not duplicate" written on them, many locksmiths will still duplicate the key. Electronic keys are the best for security purposes.

Hosts automate their check-in process in different ways. Because the Airbnb is booked through the Airbnb site, you have all the information from your guests you need. All you have to do is keep your promises and make sure they know the rules and regulations of the house. This is when a welcome book is a great tool to use. The guests can look through this book at any time to make sure they follow all the guidelines, utilize all the services, and find the best places to eat.

Use the Airbnb Management Software

There is a lot of software for Airbnb managers, and it is in your best interest to take advantage of them. Through the software, you can manage your messages, reservations, and anything else you feel is important. You can choose to see what notification you will receive right away. You can even schedule cleaning services, read your reviews, and get an idea of your rankings.

Guest Relations

One of the many benefits of using management software is the ease of communicating with your guests. The Airbnb website wants people to communicate through their site as they can help you in case you get into a bind. Plus, their site will automatically save your correspondence. Not only do you need to keep in contact with your guests before they arrive, but you need to make yourself available throughout their stay. If any problems arise, you need to take care of the issue as soon as possible. You should also want to know how their stay is going, if you can further assist them in any way, or if they need more supplies. While you always need to have your financial status in mind, going above and beyond for your guests will make sure they place you on their wishlist and leave a 5-star review.

You can also give your guests messages at any time through the management software. This will help keep your guests informed and give them a more pleasant experience. For example, you can let them know you will be in the area and would like to meet with them. You can then schedule a time so you don't have to show up unannounced. You always need to be respectful of their privacy throughout their stay.

Cleaning Team and How to Outsource Efficiently

You can use the management software to schedule a cleaning team, or you can form your own cleaning team. If you decide to use the management software, you can create a cleaning schedule for your staff. You can tell them what needs to be cleaned, and when. You can create their hours, and give them any direction on where to find cleaning supplies or how to clean certain areas of the Airbnb.

Some hosts like to use their own method with cleaning. They might hire one person to clean every day and to work certain hours. This person may also have other responsibilities, such as checking in with the guests, and managing the day-to-day operations of the Airbnb. Hosts who have several units will often hire a team to take care of each unit.

There are also hosts that like to do everything themselves. Usually, they haven't been in the business long and are still building, or they rent part of their home for extra money. These hosts tend to quickly build a relationship with their guests, and usually have good experiences and don't deal with much damage. People are less likely to cause damage if the host or staff are visible on a daily basis.

Generating 5-Star Reviews

You already have several ideas that can generate 5-star reviews. For example, you want to communicate with your guests often, give them realistic expectations, and under-promise. However, there are many other steps you can take to generate strong reviews.

- Make your listing clear and concise. This goes beyond under-promising them. You want to ensure that your guests understand your description and what your Airbnb offers. When you communicate with your guests, ask them if they have any questions and concerns.
- Always send a check-in message to welcome them to your Airbnb. You can use this time to give them the electronic key code, and remind them of the check-in process.
- When your guests come to you with a problem or concern, address them quickly and seriously. Keep the frame of mind that you need to make sure your guests have the best experience possible.
- Always send a check-out message. You can send them a message before they check out to remind them of the procedure, and ask if they have any questions or concerns. You should also send them a message after they leave. You can do this the next day or a couple of days later. During this time, you can send

them a survey about their stay and ask them to write a review and add you to their wishlist.

Chapter 13: Scaling Up the Business

Once you open your business, your first step is growing your business. It is important to remember that this will take time. You won't generate a lot of business right away, even if you are in a popular area for Airbnbs. However, there are many people who like to stay at different Airbnbs and enjoy visiting new businesses.

The biggest way to start growing your business is to make sure that you have your processes down and that you follow them thoroughly. You want to make sure that everyone understands your processes and are treated equally. Guests are honest in their reviews, and they will notice when they are treated in a different way than other guests.

Tips for Growing Your Business

By now, you already have tons of ideas to help your Airbnb business blossom. However, this is a topic where you can never get enough tips to help you start your journey. Below are a few tips that other hosts follow to grow their business.

Manage Your Risk

There is some risk that you will know when you start your business. There is also risk you will come across once you have your first few guests. Unfortunately, no matter how hard you try, you cannot prepare for everything. However, the way you handle situations will determine how strong your business becomes.

The hosts that build their Airbnbs into a six-figure salary handle every situation in a calm and rational manner. Even when they are struggling with their guests, they keep in mind that they need to be polite and respectful. At the same time, they need to make sure that they are treated fairly. They have the "customer is always right" mentality, but also include the "this is my business" mentality. If you want to run a successful business, you need to do your best to find a balance between these two mentalities. It isn't something that you will find right away. This mentality will grow over time.

One risk that you will learn to manage is noticing bad guests, such as people who are disrespectful and will damage your property. These guests can seem like your average guest, but they will often give you subtle hints that they truly don't care how they leave your Airbnb. They will throw parties and not pay attention to the rules and regulations. One way to limit these guests is to establish guidelines for your Airbnb and stick with them.

Have a Strong Business Plan

Before you open your Airbnb, you want to establish a business plan to follow. You will write down any information, rules, guidelines, and processes in this business plan. Take time to write about your goals for your Airbnb. For example, do you want to open a new unit within the next couple years? If so, this is the type of goal you want to write down. You will also want to list the steps you will take to reach this goal and give yourself a timeline.

Don't Spend Too Much Time Worrying

It is easy to get caught up worrying about ratings and reviews. However, this can make you anxious and stressed. When you are feeling this way, your mind becomes clouded and you don't make clear and rational decisions. This will cause you to make mistakes and can lead you to get bad reviews from unhappy guests.

Realize that nothing is perfect. Instead, you want to create a perfectly imperfect Airbnb business. When your guests see that you are human and trying your best to give them their best experience, they will be impressed and leave good reviews.

Don't worry about the reviews that are four stars. These are still good reviews, and will give you information for growth. Read the review and analyze what your guests are saying. Some people are going to give you a lower review, but four stars is still a great review.

Don't take their review personally. Look for information that will help you change your process if you feel the guests brought up a good point. Sometimes, your guests will notice factors that you didn't consider. This isn't bad, as it will help you become a stronger host.

Have Multiple Listings

Most hosts have one listing. This is fine if you aren't planning on growing your business. Take a moment to think about how much you need to charge your guests to make a six-figure salary every year with just one unit. Unless you have a large home, this will be difficult. Your best option to establish a strong salary is to slowly add more listing to your business. You don't want to do this all at once, as it can make you feel overwhelmed. Once you understand the business, your unit is booked, and you feel confident about adding another listing, then this is what you do.

Be Reasonable About Paying Your Staff

If you have multiple listings around the United States, you will need to hire staff to help you manage your properties. You will have managers, a cleaning team, and an accountant to take care of the bookwork.

Most hosts build up to this point within several years. However, they also find themselves struggling when it comes to paying their staff. If they underpay, they struggle to keep their staff. If they overpay, then they struggle to stay financially positive.

The best way to work around this is to research what the average rate to pay your staff. You might find that you don't need to pay your staff as much in some areas than others. For instance, the cost of living is lower in the Midwest than it is on the East or West coast. This is a factor you will want to consider. Another factor to consider is regular pay raises, the state's minimum wage, and the experience of your staff members.

Chapter 14: Mindset

One of the biggest factors when it comes to growing your business is your mindset. Your mindset will set the tone for your business and how you handle your guests. For example, if you have a positive mindset, you will bring more positivity into your guests' stay. You might give them some positive messages, make them feel more at home, and give them a better experience overall. When you have a negative mindset, you will come off as domineering, and can make your guests feel uncomfortable. A negative mindset is going to lead to negative reviews, and you will struggle to maintain your business.

Your mindset will depend on your personality, and how you feel about your Airbnb business. For instance, if you are excited and you believe that you can accomplish anything, you will radiate this type of energy. Some people are naturally confident, while others need to build their confidence. Before we go any further, it is important for you to understand where your self-confidence sits at this moment.

Take a minute to reflect on how you feel about starting your Airbnb journey. Do you believe that you can build an amazing empire, or you do think that your business will struggle because you don't know if you have the necessary skills to run a successful business? This can be a difficult exercise for some people, but it is necessary to see where you sit on a psychological level, so you can utilize the mindset tips to help your confidence and business grow.

The Winning Mindset

The winning mindset is exactly how it sounds. You believe you are winning. You believe that you are building a strong Airbnb empire, and that you will reach all of your goals. There is nothing holding you back. You are intelligent, possess amazing skills, and you know how to keep your guest relations strong. You know that you will gain 5-star reviews and make it as one of the top hosts on the Airbnb website. This is known as a confident person with the winning mindset. This is the type of mindset you want. Don't worry if you feel you need to work on your mindset as most people do. Fortunately, there are a lot of tips that can help you in this process.

Maintain a Calm Environment

Your mindset starts in your home. This is something that a lot of people don't think about because they try to separate their personal life and work life. This is something that can help you but harm you at the same time. For instance, you can't have the winning mindset at your job and have a poor mindset at home. You need to take your winning mindset everywhere. This means that you need to build and maintain your mindset throughout the day.

Many people like to start their day off with an inspirational message or meditation. This helps them set their tone for the day, which helps them maintain a calm environment. The key is to remain consistent with this process. For example, if you decide to meditate every morning, do it every morning. This will help keep your mindset and make you calmer over time.

Have a Passion to Succeed

Don't hide your passion when it comes to what you want. Write down your goals and do everything in your power to make them happen. The most successful Airbnb hosts have one thing in common, and that is their passion to succeed. With this passion, they remain dedicated, work through any obstacles, and do what they need to in order to maintain a strong relationship with their guests.

If you don't have passion for your Airbnb, you are in the wrong area. Even if you have a passion for investing in real estate, there are different areas you can invest in. If you don't feel that Airbnb is your interest, look into apartment complexes or flipping homes.

You are Always Looking for Ways to Grow

You might feel that you are putting too much effort into your business at times. While you do want to find a healthy balance between your business and personal life, putting forth so much effort isn't bad. In fact, it shows that you want to succeed, and that you are looking for ways to grow your business. For example, if you receive a bad review, you will look at this review as a way to grow. You will note what the reviewer stated and look through your policies, procedures, and identify ways you can change the situation so it doesn't affect another guest. You may even contact the guest who left the bad review and tell them what changes you are making.

You Watch Your Spending

You want your guests to have the best, but you also understand your budget. You are not going to risk your business to give your guests satin bed sheets. You are going to make sure you have quality items, but also watch the price. You understand that some of your best decor you will find in the clearance section, and this is fine. If it matches your Airbnb, is clean, and can give your unit more appeal, then you find a great item for the best price! Never assume that you have to spend hundreds of dollars to make your Airbnb look its best. You can find the same item for $20 with a little patience.

Monitor the Progress of Your Goals

You will write your goals down and the step-by-step process for them when you establish your business plan. However, you also need to monitor the progress on your goals. You need to keep a journal where you can look back on any day and note how far you have come. This is a great step in maintaining your winning mindset, because you can look back at your progress after a bad day, or when you are mentally struggling. You can note how far you have come and be proud of yourself. This is an important step in the winning mindset. You always need to be proud of your accomplishments.

Always Think Positively

Always maintaining a positive attitude is challenging. There is a lot of negativity in this world, and thinking negatively brings more negativity. Think of your attitude like a magnet. When you are positive, you will pull in positivity into your life. When you are negative, you will pull in negativity into your life. Therefore, the more positive you are, the stronger your winning mindset.

If you find yourself in a challenging situation, look at the positives. For example, with a negative review, you can think: *This is helpful because it will allow me to grow as a host.* If you don't have any guests in your Airbnb for a week, you can think: *This is great. I can take this time to do some deep cleaning and go through the unit to make any updates.*

Surround Yourself with Like-Minded People

You want to look for people who think positively and have the winning mindset in other hosts. You can meet hosts through the Airbnb site or by looking in your local phonebook. Don't consider other hosts as enemies because of the competitive market. You can make friends with the hosts and help your business grow. Furthermore, you can talk to them about any struggles and get advice from hosts who have been in the business for a while. There are a lot of experienced hosts who are willing to help a beginner through the first stages and see them grow. The less you see other hosts as a threat, the more positive your mindset will become.

Unfortunately, there is no quick way to develop the winning mindset. You have to go slowly and remain mindful of your thoughts. This means that you recognize your thoughts and can turn negative thoughts into positive ones. Once we start to feel bad about a situation, we begin to feel bad about ourselves. This leads us to a poor mindset, which is hard to switch off if we don't catch the negativity right away.

If you do struggle with confidence, one tip to follow is to place positive messages in your office, home, car, or wherever you deem appropriate. You don't need to write elaborate messages. You can write, "You got this!" "You are doing great!" or "You are on top of the world! Keep going!" Place them in random locations where you will see them every day.

Another tip is to create a visualization board. This is when you will think of the goals you want to achieve over the year and find pictures that correlate with these goals. For example, if you want to open your second Airbnb, you will have a picture of an Airbnb. Place the visualization board where you will see it every day and take time to analyze the board. The more you visualize your goals, the more likely you are to succeed. The main reason for this is because your mind believes that you are capable of reaching your goals.

One of the biggest factors to maintaining the winning mindset is you have to be consistent. Even if you wake up on the wrong side of the bed, take time to look at your daily affirmations and meditate. Follow your schedule as this will help you switch any negativity into positivity.

Another factor is to always remember to be kind to yourself. Even when you make a mistake, use this as a learning opportunity and room for growth. Don't give up because of the mistake, and don't talk down to yourself. Be gentle, just as you would with anyone else. As you build your winning mindset, you will spread this positivity to those around you. This will make your guests more comfortable, and you will make their wishlist. You will receive good reviews, and they will want to come back and recommend you to their friends.

Conclusion

Even though Airbnb investing is a new type of investing, it is growing and there is a lot of potential in this market. There are dozens of benefits of Airbnb investing, such as: Expanding into other locations, growing your wealth, meeting people from all over the world, and having an automated system. You can stay on top of your units and make sure that your guests are having a positive experience.

These benefits don't mean there aren't risks associated with this type of renting. There are several ways to limit your risks. For example, by making your Airbnb safe, you will keep your guests, neighbors, and yourself safe. You can start to learn the red flags of bad tenants, and learn the tricks to avoid the risk of vacancy.

You know how to handle the competition and realize that it's not bad. While it can make it harder to get noticed by guests, you will find what makes your Airbnb stand out from the rest. You have the knowledge to write a compelling description and understand the importance of pictures. All these factors will help launch your Airbnb business into the top rankings of the Airbnb website.

You also know of several tips to help you receive a higher ranking. You have knowledge of how the algorithms on the Airbnb site work and what to keep in mind. For instance, you understand the importance of reviews and communicating with your guests. These are two of the most important factors when it comes to high rankings.

This guide also helped you learn how to receive these higher rankings. You know what to pay attention to when you are picking out furniture for your unit. You know to spend time researching for the perfect location. You can form your welcome book to make sure your guests understand the process and feel welcomed to your Airbnb, even when you aren't around to welcome them yourself.

You have a clear understanding of the expenses when it comes to Airbnb investing. For example, you know of the obvious expenses, such as bills and repairs, but you also know about the hidden expenses.

Part of Airbnb investing starts when you are renting the unit. In this case, you have to gain permission from your landlord and ensure that you are on the same page before you start the process. This can take time, but through this guide, you can overcome your worry and speak honestly and confidently with your landlord. You can also use this mindset to reach your neighbors and help them understand Airbnb investing and how this will not affect their lives negatively. You have the tools to help everyone feel at ease with your plan.

Above all, you understand the importance of the winning mindset and how this will help you gain control over your life, especially as a host. Even if you don't have this mindset now, through the tips in this book, you can build this mindset and realize your full potential. With your passion to succeed, you will build the Airbnb empire that you visualize.

Don't stop now, as you have only started to live your dream! Use the tips, exercises, and tools from this book to help you reach your goals. Take time and don't rush through the process as you want to do your best. As long as you are working hard and believe in yourself, you will soon open your first Airbnb and start seeing your empire grow.

You may also like these books:

Real Estate Investing Through Tax Liens &
Deeds: The Beginner's Guide To Earning
Sustainable A Passive Income While Reducing
Risks (Traditional Buy & Hold Doesn't Work
Anymore)

Blogging For Profit: The No Nonsense Beginner's Blueprint To Earn Money Online With Your Blog

Badass Passive Income Ideas That Your Teacher Won't Tell You: Multiple Income Streams (Both Online And Offline) That Will Help You Achieve Financial Freedom And Money Goals

References

10 Unique Tips to Ranking Among Airbnb's Best Listings. (2018). Retrieved 13 October 2019, from https://www.igms.com/airbnb-best-listings/

Airbnb Search Results: 10 Tips to Improve Your Ranking. (2019). Retrieved 13 October 2019, from https://www.lodgify.com/blog/airbnb-search-results/

Barzilay, O. (2017). 10 Things To Consider Before Buying An Airbnb Investment. Retrieved 12 October 2019, from https://www.forbes.com/sites/omribarzilay/2017/04/04/things-to-consider-before-buying-an-airbnb-investment/#71d386b14869

Fishman, S. How to Prepare Your Home for Airbnb, VRBO, or Other Short-Term Guests. Retrieved 12 October 2019, from https://www.nolo.com/legal-encyclopedia/how-prepare-your-home-airbnb-vrbo-other-short-term-guests.html

How can I prepare to host? Retrieved 12 October 2019, from https://www.airbnb.com/help/article/1189/how-can-i-prepare-to-host

How do I activate my listing? Retrieved 13 October 2019, from https://www.airbnb.com/help/article/883/how-do-i-activate-my-listing

How should I talk to my landlord about hosting on Airbnb? Retrieved 12 October 2019, from https://www.airbnb.com/help/article/806/how-should-i-talk-to-my-landlord-about-hosting-on-airbnb

Khoury, M. (2018). 7 Risks of an Airbnb Property Investment and How to Overcome Them. Retrieved 12 October 2019, from https://www.mashvisor.com/blog/7-risks-airbnb-property-investment-how-to-overcome-them/

Leasca, S. (2017). https://www.travelandleisure.com. Retrieved 11 October 2019, from https://www.travelandleisure.com/travel-tips/how-much-airbnb-hosts-make

Ribek, C. (2018). To Furnish or Not to Furnish Your Rental Property. Retrieved 12 October 2019, from https://www.mashvisor.com/blog/furnish-rental-property/

Saldana, M. (2019). Which US Cities Are the Best (and Worst) for Rental Arbitrage on Airbnb and HomeAway? Retrieved 12 October 2019, from https://www.airdna.co/blog/best-worst-rental-arbitrage-airbnb-homeaway

Smith, A. (2018). Airbnb: How to Make a Six-Figure Income Without Owning Any Property. Kindle Edition.

Top 5 photo tips for a stellar listing. Retrieved 13 October 2019, from https://blog.atairbnb.com/top-5-photo-tips-for-a-stellar-listing/

What are profile verifications and how do I get them? Retrieved 11 October 2019, from https://www.airbnb.com/help/article/336/what-are-profile-verifications-and-how-do-i-get-them

What factors determine how my listing appears in search results? Retrieved 12 October 2019, from https://www.airbnb.com/help/article/39/what-factors-determine-how-my-listing-appears-in-search-results

What is Airbnb and how does it work? Retrieved 11 October 2019, from https://www.airbnb.com/help/article/2503/what-is-airbnb-and-how-does-it-work

What Is Airbnb Insurance? Retrieved 12 October 2019, from https://www.valuepenguin.com/what-is-airbnb-insurance#airbnb-renters

What is Instant Book? Retrieved 13 October 2019, from
https://www.airbnb.com/help/article/523/what-is-instant-book

Why should I pay and communicate through Airbnb directly? Retrieved 11 October 2019, from
https://www.airbnb.com/help/article/209/why-should-i-pay-and-communicate-through-airbnb-directly

Printed in Great Britain
by Amazon